The Big 5-0

Other For Better or For Worse® Collections

Retrospectives

The Big 5-0

A *For Better or For Worse*® Collection
by Lynn Johnston

Andrews McMeel
Publishing

Kansas City

01 02 03 BAH 10 9 8 7 6 5 4 3 2

ISBN: 0-7407-0556-3

Library of Congress Catalog Card Number: 00-103476

──── **ATTENTION: SCHOOLS AND BUSINESSES** ────

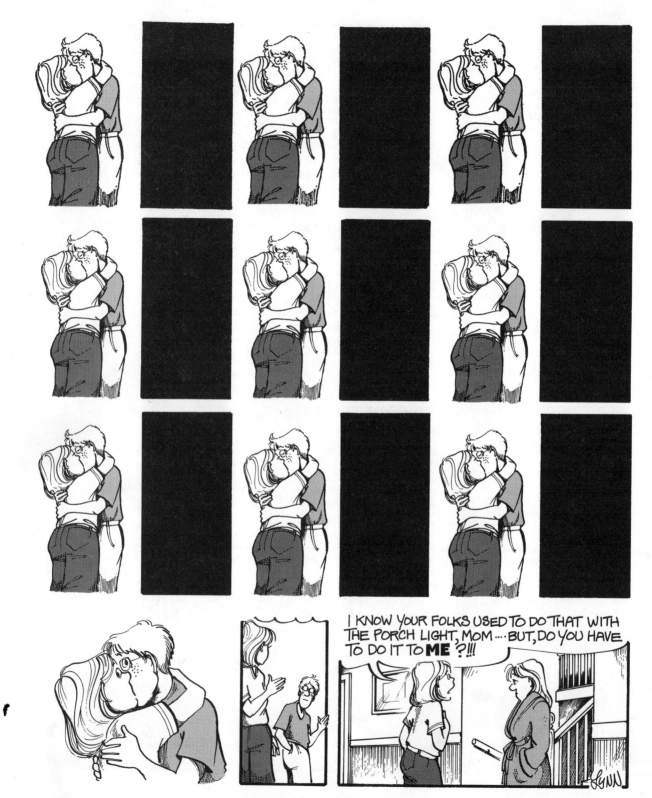

14

15

Panel 1: SO WHAT'D YOU DO ALL SUMMER, LIZ? / WE WENT OUT WEST WITH MY GRANDFATHER FOR A COUPLE OF WEEKS....

Panel 2: THEN I WORKED AT MEGAFOOD WHEN WE GOT BACK — HOW ABOUT YOU, DUANE? / SLRRK

Panel 3: WELL, UH... I DID STUFF FOR MY DAD, MOSTLY.

Panel 4: FOR SOME REASON I HAD A TOUGH TIME GETTIN' A JOB!

Panel 5: YEAH, IT WAS A WEIRD SUMMER. I SAW CANDACE A LOT — SHE GOT A TATTOO ON HER HEAD. ...A CROWN OF THORNS! NOW SHE'S LETTIN' HER HAIR GROW BACK.

Panel 6: HER MOM'S NEW BOYFRIEND IS A FREAK, SO SHE'S MOVED IN WITH HER DAD AGAIN — AN' MY MOM KICKED ME OUTTA THE HOUSE FOR GETTIN' A NIPPLE RING ...SO I'M LIVIN' IN OUR GARAGE.

Panel 7: WE CAN'T WAIT TO GO TO UNIVERSITY NEXT YEAR AN' GET AWAY FROM HERE!

Panel 8: WHAT DO YOU GUYS WANT TO BE, DUANE? / PSYCHOLOGISTS.

Panel 9: SO, HOW'S GRADE 13 SO FAR, LIZ? / OK... EVERYONE'S GETTING SERIOUS ABOUT THEIR FUTURE, SO IT'S COOL FINDING OUT WHAT THEY WANNA BE.

Panel 10: WHAT DO YOU WANNA BE, ELIZABETH? / A TEACHER, BECAUSE OF MISS EDWARDS. SHE WAS SO EXCELLENT... AN' I JUST WANNA BE LIKE HER.

Panel 11: YES, THERE WERE A NUMBER OF WONDERFUL TEACHERS IN MY LIFE, TOO ....AND, IF I PUT MY MIND TO IT — I CAN REMEMBER EVERY ONE!

Panel 12: SIGH — KNOW WHAT, DADDY? ..... SO CAN I.

27

YE'VE COME TO SEE US 'BOUT COLM O'CONNOR, 'AVE YE? — THAT'S 'IM... PAINTED BY 'IS WIFE, REBECCA.

HE WAS 15 YEARS OLD WHEN 'E COME TO CANADA BY COFFIN SHIP — THAT'S WHAT THEY WAS CALLED. ...SAILED FROM LIMERICK, IRELAND, IN 1845, WITH 300 SOULS ABOARD. WHEN SHE PUT INTO PORT ...'E WAS THE ONLY ONE WHAT MADE IT.

THERE WAS 'IM, THE CAPTAIN OF THE SHIP AN' TWO MATES. THE OTHERS ALL PERISHED.

IN T'OSE DAYS, IF YOU SURVIVED THE VOYAGE, YOU'D SAILED FIRST CLASS.

COLM O'CONNOR WAS QUARANTINED FOR SOME WEEKS ON GROSSE ILE, THEN SET FREE ON THE MAINLAND TO FEND FER HISSELF.

HE WORKED 'IS WAY DOWN RIVER AND AN ENGLISH LANDOWNER TOOK 'IM AN' 'AD 'IM WORK ON THIS VERY HOUSE!

MUCH OF THIS STONE WAS CUT AN' SET BY 'IS OWN TWO HANDS.

HE WAS A MASON?

HE WAS A SLAVE.

OH, YES, ME SONS. — WE WERE NOT AT ALL WELCOME HERE IN CANADA — NOR IN THE STATES TO THE SOUTH.

IT WAS BAD LUCK FER BOTH THE IRISH AN' THE FRENCH, WHERE ENGLAND RULED THE ROOST!

COLM O'CONNOR WAS AN UNPAID LABORER TO THE OWNER OF THIS HOUSE... UNTIL THE PARISH PRIEST TOOK 'IM IN. SAVED 'IS LIFE ...AN' TAUGHT 'IM HOW TO PLAY THE FIDDLE.

...IS THIS....?

'OLD'ER IN YOUR HANDS, MR. PATTERSON. — THE BEAT OF 'IS HEART IS STILL IN 'ER.

COLM O'CONNOR SURVIVED THE POTATO FAMINE, THE COFFIN SHIP AND FORCED LABOR TO BECOME ONE O' THE FINEST MUSICIANS IRELAND EVER PRODUCED.

HE MARRIED AN ENGLISH WOMAN, LEARNED HOW TO READ AN' WRITE—AND EVENTUALLY, HE ACQUIRED SOME LAND!

LAND! NOW, THAT WAS A RARE T'ING IN THOSE DAYS. A MAN LIKE 'IM OWNING 'IS OWN LAND!

IT WAS HARD TO GET THE MONEY?

IT WAS HARD TO GET THE RIGHT!

COLM AND REBECCA 'AD A SON WHO WAS ALLOWED AN EDUCATION BECAUSE 'IS MOTHER WAS ENGLISH AN' 'IS FATHER 'AD MADE A NAME FER HIMSELF.

THE SON BUILT A GOOD BUSINESS AN' SO IT WENT... AN' ALL THE WHILE, THE FAMILY SAW THIS HOUSE AS BELONGING TO COLM O'CONNOR.

THIS MONTH, FOUR GENERATIONS AFTER 'E LEFT THIS EARTH, 'IS STONE HOUSE 'AS COME BACK TO HIM... —WE JUST BOUGHT HER!

AN' WHEN WE DID, 'TWAS THE FIRST TIME WE NOTICED— THAT PAINTING OF 'IM 'AD A SMILE ON 'ER.

SO, THE STONE HOUSE COLM O'CONNOR BUILT NEARLY 150 YEARS AGO NOW BELONGS TO THE O'CONNOR CLAN!

SOME OF US ARE IN NEW-FOUNDLAND, LABRADOR, NOVA SCOTIA AND MAINE. THE REST ARE RIGHT HERE IN QUEBEC.

AND HOW DO THEY FEEL ABOUT ALL OF THIS?

YE CAN ASK 'EM Y'SELF, LAD...

THEY'RE HERE!

Panel 1:
ALL OF THESE PEOPLE ARE RELATIVES?
ALL THOSE WHO COULD MAKE IT HERE TODAY.

Panel 2:
IT'S GOING TO BE A REUNION, THANKS TO YOU!
WE JUST CAME TO DO A STORY ABOUT YOUR HOUSE. WE DIDN'T EXPECT TO STAY FOR A PARTY!—

Panel 3:
WELL, THE TRUTH OF IT IS— IT'S GOOD LUCK IF YOU INVITE SOME STRANGERS TO A CELEBRATION...

Panel 4:
SO WE TOOK A LOOK AT THE LIKES OF YOU, AN' THOUGHT YOU WERE STRANGE ENOUGH!

Panel 5:
THIS IS COOL, MIKE. I'VE NEVER BEEN TO A SHINDIG LIKE THIS BEFORE!
NEITHER HAVE I.

Panel 6:
MOST OF THE PEOPLE HERE SPEAK FRENCH— AND SOME SPEAK GAELIC AS WELL!
LOOK— MR. O'CONNOR'S SON IS TAKING HIS GREAT, GREAT GRANDFATHER'S VIOLIN OUT OF THE CABINET.

Panel 7:
C'EST L'TEMPS!—IT'S TIME!

Panel 8:
WE DEDICATE THIS HOUSE TO TH' MAN WHO BUILT 'ER. MAY HIS SPIRIT DANCE AS HIS FIDDLE PLAYS.

Panel 9:
WHAT A SWEET MELODY. EXCEPT FOR THE SOUND OF COLM O'CONNOR'S VIOLIN... YOU COULD HEAR A PIN DROP.

Panel 10:
....IT'S AS IF HIS GHOST HAD JUST ENTERED THE ROOM.

Panel 11:
AND IF HE COULD SPEAK— I WONDER WHAT HE'D SAY AT THIS POINT IN TIME!

Panel 12:
DRINK UP, ME SON! MAY THE JOYS OF TODAY BE THOSE OF TOMORROW! MAY THY GOBLET OF LIFE HOLD NO DREGS OF SORROW!!

40

RRRRRRRr

APRIL! – I FINISHED YOUR HALLOWE'EN COSTUME!

BUT, I DON'T WANNA BE BO-PEEP!

YOU SAID YOU WANTED TO BE A STORYBOOK CHARACTER THIS YEAR!

THAT'S 'CAUSE BECKY WAS GONNA BE RED RIDING HOOD– BUT, SHE CHANGED HER MIND!

NOW, WE WANNA BE SPICE GIRLS!

IT'S TOO LATE TO BE A SPICE GIRL.

I DON'T WANNA BE A STORYBOOK CHARACTER UNLESS SOMEBODY'S GONNA BE A STORY-BOOK CHARACTER **WITH** ME !!!

TRICK OR TREAT

A FEW MONTHS AGO I STEPPED OUTSIDE, AND THIS PRETTY LITTLE DOG WAS JUST SITTING THERE.

I KNEW SHE LIVED TWO CONDOS DOWN, SO I TOOK HER HOME. THE NEXT MORNING SHE WAS BACK—SITTING OUTSIDE MY DOOR.

IT'S AS IF SHE KNEW SHE WAS GOING TO BE LIVING WITH ME—WHY ELSE WOULD SHE BE THERE?!!

WERE YOU FRYING BACON?

DAD, I'M SO GLAD YOU HAVE A DOG NOW.

YES. DIXIE HAS QUITE THE PERSONALITY!

AND SHE LOVES TO RUN. I TAKE HER TO THE PARK AND I THROW STICKS FOR HER. SHE LOVES THAT!

I'M TELLING YOU, ELLY—THIS LITTLE DOG GIVES ME A REASON TO GET UP EVERY MORNING.

...ESPECIALLY IF SHE'S HAD A LOT TO DRINK THE NIGHT BEFORE!

I'M GOING TO MAKE IT, EL. I'M GOING TO SURVIVE ON MY OWN.

EVERY DAY I'M A LITTLE MORE CONFIDENT. EVERY DAY I'M A LITTLE MORE CHEERFUL.

AND YOU HAVE COMPANY NOW, DAD!

YES. DIXIE IS A BRIGHT DOG.

IT'S TAKING LESS TIME FOR HER TO TRAIN ME THAN I THOUGHT IT WOULD!!

47

50

Panel 1: THIS PROF. IS GOING ON AN' ON... AND SHE LOST ME COMPLETELY ABOUT 15 MINUTES AGO.

Panel 2: EVERYONE ELSE SEEMS TO UNDERSTAND. I MUST BE THE ONLY ONE HERE WHO'S CONFUSED!

Panel 3: I REALLY WANT HER TO STOP AND GO OVER SOME OF THIS STUFF AGAIN.

Panel 4: BUT IF I PUT UP MY HAND, 175 PEOPLE WILL THINK I'M A DOOFUS!

LYNN

Panel 5: MICHAEL, CAN I GET YOUR NOTES FROM THAT LAST LECTURE?
SURE, BUT I STOPPED WRITING WHEN I FELL ASLEEP.

Panel 6: JORGE TAPED IT, SO WE CAN MAKE COPIES OF THE ENTIRE LECTURE DOWN IN A.V. SERVICES.
COOL!

Panel 7: AUDIO VISUAL SERVICES

Panel 8: AND BY COMPARING THE PRELIMINARY OUTLINE TO THE ROUGH FIRST DRAFT WE CONCLUDE THAT THE UTILIZATION OF PARENTHESIS AND FIRST PERSON SINGULAR ARE NOW SIGNIFICANT FUNDAMENTAL ELEMENTS....
SNWARRKK!

LYNN

Panel 9: MIKE! MIKE! CHECK IT OUT! OUR ARTICLE MADE THE DECEMBER ISSUE OF PORTRAIT MAGAZINE!
UH?

Panel 10: THAT MEANS WE GET PAID, MAN! THESE GUYS PAY ON PUBLICATION. I THOUGHT WE'D HAFTA WAIT FOR 90 DAYS OR SOMETHING!
LEMME SEE THAT!

Panel 11: WOW. OUR FIRST COMMISSION — IT LOOKS GOOD, WEED!...CAN I BORROW THIS?
SURE! - I FIGURED YOU'D WANT TO KEEP THAT COPY.

Panel 12: .... SO I PICKED UP A FEW MORE.

LYNN

WE DID A GOOD JOB ON THIS ARTICLE, WEED—I HOPE THE PEOPLE WE INTERVIEWED ARE HAPPY WITH IT.

THEY ARE, MIKE—AN' BETTER THAN THAT! SO ARE THE GUYS AT THE MAGAZINE. THEY WANT US TO DO MORE STUFF.

YOU'RE SERIOUS—?

YEE-HAW!

WHOAA!!

YOU KNOW, PATTERSON—THE TROUBLE WITH YOU IS THAT YOU NEVER SHOW YOUR EMOTIONS.

THIS IS OUR FIRST BIG BREAK, DEANNA! THIS MEANS I *CAN* MAKE MY LIVING AS A WRITER!!

I KNEW THAT!

I'M SO HAPPY, I CAN'T STAND IT!!!

MICHAEL, LET'S CELEBRATE!

I **AM** CELEBRATING!

NO, REALLY—LET'S GET SOME PEOPLE TOGETHER.

SOME PEOPLE **ARE** TOGETHER!

COULD YOU BE SERIOUS FOR JUST ONE MINUTE?!

SURE...LET'S PICK A TIME NEXT WEEK!

UH, MRS. DINGLE? THE WEED AN' I ARE HAVING A FEW PEOPLE OVER FOR A PARTY. IS THAT O K?

HOW MANY PEOPLE?

JUST A FEW CLOSE FRIENDS.

I DON'T KNOW. I'M NOT TOO THRILLED. YOU MAY BE RENTIN', BUT IT'S MY HOUSE—AN' I NEEDS MY SLEEP.

BUT IT'S A CELEBRATION!

I DON'T CARE IF IT'S A FLIPPIN' **WAKE!**—YOU LOT ARE GOIN' TO BE UP 'TIL THE WEE HOURS, AN' THER'S ONLY **ONE** WAY I'LL ALLOW IT TO HAPPEN!

CONGRATULATIONS ON YOUR FIRST PUBLISHED WORK, BOYS!

HEAR-EAR!

YO!

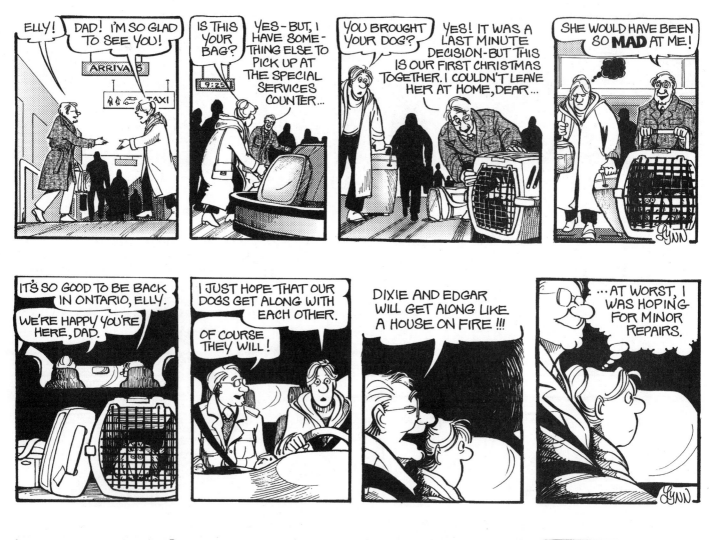

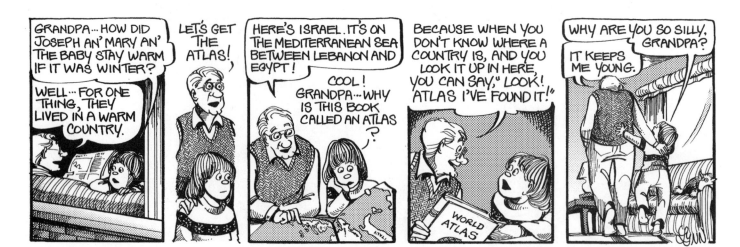

MAN, WE'VE BEEN HERE SO LONG, THE WINDOWS HAVE FOGGED OVER!

IT WON'T WIPE OFF! IT'S FROZEN!

CHIP CHIP CHIP!

SCRAPE

SCRATCH

...AT LEAST YOU KNEW WHERE I WAS!

Panel 1: DO YOU HAVE ANY "GRANNY FEELINGS" YET, EL? / NO. I DON'T THINK SO.

Panel 2: MY ELDEST STEPDAUGHTER IS MARRIED NOW, AND ALL I THINK ABOUT IS— WHEN ARE THEY GOING TO GIVE US GRANDCHILDREN?

Panel 3: I SEE BABIES IN CARRIAGES, AND I GO BY CHILDREN'S STORES AND I WISH I HAD SOMEONE TO BUY FOR.

Panel 4: I GUESS THAT EXPLAINS THE HAT AND JACKET.

Panel 5: ANY TALK OF MIKE AND DEANNA GETTING MARRIED, EL? / NOT YET, THANK GOODNESS!

Panel 6: THEY'RE NOT READY TO SETTLE DOWN, CONNIE. THEY NEED A CHANCE TO DEVELOP THEIR CAREERS AND ENJOY THEIR FREEDOM.

Panel 7: PEOPLE DON'T GET MARRIED SO YOUNG ANYMORE—AND THEY WAIT TO HAVE CHILDREN. KIDS TODAY HAVE PLENTY OF TIME! / I KNOW...

Panel 8: BUT WE DON'T.

Panel 9: YOU SURPRISE ME, CONNIE. THIS IS THE FIRST TIME I'VE HEARD YOU SAY YOU WANTED TO BE A GRANDPARENT!

Panel 10: I KNOW. SUDDENLY, "THOSE FEELINGS" JUST STARTED TO COME OVER ME.

Panel 11: WHAT HAVE YOU BEEN DOING, WATCHING THE CALENDAR? / NOPE...

Panel 12: ...I'VE BEEN WATCHING YOUR DAD.

Panel 1: NOW WHAT ARE YOU DOING?
WONDERING HOW I'D LOOK WITHOUT WRINKLES.

Panel 2: I'VE GOT MORE WRINKLES THAN YOU HAVE! BUT... MEN LOOK GOOD WHEN THEY GET OLDER. MATURE MEN HAVE A SORT OF RUGGED HANDSOMENESS.

Panel 3: I THINK OLDER MEN ARE EXTREMELY ATTRACTIVE.

Panel 4: AS LONG AS THEY'RE CLOTHED

Panel 5: GOOD MORNING, DR. P! — I JUST NOTICED ON THE CALENDAR THAT YOUR 50TH BIRTHDAY'S COMING UP!

Panel 6: REALLY? TO TELL YOU THE TRUTH, I HADN'T GIVEN IT MUCH THOUGHT, JEAN.

Panel 7: AS FAR AS I'M CONCERNED, YOU'RE ONLY AS OLD AS YOU FEEL!

Panel 8: CRAACK!

Panel 9: 50 ISN'T SO BAD, JOHN. I'LL BE 50 IN A YEAR OR SO AND LOOK AT ME! I CAN STILL PICK UP A BABE IN A BAR!

Panel 10: YOU'VE JUST GOTTA LOOK AFTER YOURSELF, STAY IN THE GROOVE! NOBODY SAYS "IN THE GROOVE" ANY MORE, TED... IT'S "IN THE DEMO."

Panel 11: IN THE... DEMO? IN THE DEMOGRAPHIC. IF YOU'RE YOUNG AND COOL AND COMPUTER-SAVVY, YOU'RE "IN THE DEMO."

Panel 12: A WHOLE NEW LANGUAGE IS HAPPENING OUT THERE! ARE YOU READY TO ORDER?

Panel 13: ¿HABLAS ESPAÑOL?

Panel 1: YOU'RE AMAZING! YOU JUST MADE A PASS AT A GIRL WHO'S YOUNG ENOUGH TO BE... MY DAUGHTER!

Panel 2: DON'T YOU GET TIRED OF PLAYING THE FIELD?

NOT AS LONG AS THE GRASS IS GREENER SOMEWHERE ELSE!

Panel 3: BESIDES... I HAVE BEEN MORE OR LESS DEVOTED TO ONE WOMAN FOR A GREAT MANY YEARS NOW.

Panel 4: YOUR MOTHER'S OVER 80, TED.

YES... BUT SHE CAN STILL COOK!

Panel 5: YES, I'VE HAD OPPORTUNITIES TO MARRY, JOHN. BUT I'M IN NO RUSH. BESIDES, I LOVE THE CHASE, IF YOU KNOW WHAT I MEAN.

Panel 6: AND I'M VERY PARTICULAR. I CAN TELL RIGHT AWAY IF A WOMAN IS WORTH SPENDING TIME WITH. IF SHE PASSES THE FIRST TEST, THEN WE GO ON TO PHASE II.

Panel 7: WHAT'S THE FIRST TEST... SHE HAS TO MATCH YOU IN INTELLIGENCE?

Panel 8: SHE HAS TO LOOK GOOD IN MY CAR.

Panel 9: I HAD LUNCH WITH TED TODAY.

TED McCAULAY? THE GUY WHO STILL LIVES WITH HIS MOTHER? – I SEE HIM AROUND!

Panel 10: HE'S 50-ISH, GREYING HAIR – I REMEMBER, LIKE FOREVER AGO, WHEN HE DATED MOM'S FRIEND CONNIE!

Panel 11: HE'S A DOCTOR, RIGHT? AN' HE DOES FAMILY COUNSELING! KNOW WHAT? HE WAS IN A BAR ON 3RD STREET SATURDAY - TRYING TO PICK UP A GIRL WHO'S 20!! DOESN'T THAT MAKE YOU FREAK?!

Panel 12: WHAT WERE YOU DOING IN A BAR ON 3RD STREET?!

Panel 1: ANSWER YOUR MOM, LIZ. WERE YOU IN A BAR ON SATURDAY?
UH...WE WENT INTO THE WINDSOR ARMS HOTEL.

Panel 2: I WAS WITH ANTHONY AND SOME OTHER KIDS, BUT, HEY!—IT WAS JUST TO PLAY A LITTLE SNOOKER!

Panel 3: AND YOUR FRIEND TED WAS LIKE, PUTTING THE MOVES ON GIRLS **MY** AGE!

Panel 4: HOW CAN A GUY WITH SO MUCH EDUCATION AND SO MUCH EXPERIENCE BE SUCH A **JERK!**

Panel 5: ...OUT OF THE MOUTHS OF "BABES"

Panel 6: I DON'T LIKE ELIZABETH GOING INTO THE WINDSOR ARMS HOTEL, JOHN.
THE SNOOKER TABLES AREN'T IN THE BAR, EL.

Panel 7: BESIDES...THE FACT THAT SHE TOLD US SHE WENT IN THERE IS A GOOD THING. IT MEANS SHE KNOWS WE TRUST HER.

Panel 8: AND IT'S NICE TO KNOW THAT WE'VE GIVEN HER THE CONFIDENCE, DISCIPLINE AND THE JUDGMENT TO MAKE GOOD DECISIONS WHEN SHE'S IN A PLACE LIKE THAT.

Panel 9: I DON'T LIKE ELIZABETH GOING INTO THE WINDSOR ARMS HOTEL, JOHN.
...NEITHER DO I.

Panel 10: SO ELIZABETH SAW TED McCAULAY, DID SHE? I OFTEN THINK ABOUT HIM!

Panel 11: I WAS ONCE SO CRAZY ABOUT HIM, EL...AND THERE HE IS, STILL SINGLE, STILL OUT ON THE PROWL.

Panel 12: I WONDER WHAT IT WOULD HAVE BEEN LIKE IF I'D MARRIED HIM INSTEAD OF GREG.
PURE MISERY.

Panel 13: YEAH...BUT I CAN DREAM, CAN'T I?

ELIZABETH SAW TED IN A BAR, CONNIE! SHE SAID SHE WAS IN AN-OTHER ROOM PLAYING SNOOKER WITH FRIENDS.

BUT IF THAT'S SO... HOW DID SHE SEE TED McCAULAY?

COME ON, EL. SHE'S DRINK-ING AGE!

NOT YET!

=TSK= THE WINDSOR ARMS HOTEL! IS THAT SEEDY OLD FLEA PIT STILL POPULAR? WE USED TO GO THERE WHEN WE WERE KIDS — IT DROVE MY MOTHER **CRAZY!**

OH.

I DON'T WANT MY DAUGHTER HANGING AROUND THE WINDSOR ARMS HOTEL.

AS LONG AS SHE'S WITH FRIENDS, SHE'LL BE OK.

SHE WASN'T EXACTLY **IN** THE BAR, EL.

I WANT TO BELIEVE THAT, CONNIE.

BUT SOME OF THE KIDS SHE HANGS OUT WITH ARE LEGAL DRINKING AGE! WHAT'S TO KEEP HER FROM BORROWING SOME-ONE'S I.D. AND GOING IN FOR A DRINK? WELL? I DID! DIDN'T YOU?!!

I REFUSE TO ANSWER THAT ON THE GROUNDS THAT I MAY INFURIATE MYSELF.

ELIZABETH IS A GOOD KID. IF THE WINDSOR ARMS HOTEL IS THE WORST PLACE SHE GOES WITH HER FRIENDS, YOU'VE GOT NOTHING TO WORRY ABOUT.

KIDS NEED TO SEE "THE OTHER SIDE". IT'S FUN TO GO INTO A RUN-DOWN OLD PLACE AND TAKE IN THE ATMOSPHERE!

ATMOSPHERE? HMPH!!

TROUBLE IS, YOU SEE YOUR DAUGHTER AS AN INNOCENT LITTLE GIRL, AND SHE'S GROWN UP, EL. SHE'S OUT THERE. SHE'S EXPERI-MENTING. SHE'S FINDING THINGS OUT FOR HER-SELF.

CONNIE... HOW MUCH DO YOU THINK SHE KNOWS?

Panel 1: YOU TOLD YOUR MOM WE WERE AT THE WINDSOR ARMS PUB?!!
I NEVER SAID WE WENT IN... I JUST NEVER SAID WE DIDN'T.

Panel 2: MAN, YOUR PARENTS WON'T LET US GO OUT ANYMORE IF...
I'M ALMOST 18, ANTHONY. I'LL BE LEGAL IN ANOTHER YEAR, SO IT'S NO BIG DEAL!

Panel 3: I CAN'T BELIEVE HOW MUCH YOU TELL YOUR PARENTS!!
I DON'T TELL THEM **EVERYTHING!**

Panel 4: I JUST TRUTHFULLY ANSWER THE QUESTIONS THEY ASK... AND HOPE THEY DON'T ASK CERTAIN QUESTIONS.

Panel 5: ELIZABETH...COULD I TALK TO YOU PRIVATELY?
SURE, MOM— WHAT'S UP?

Panel 6: I REALLY DON'T WANT YOU TO GO INTO THE BARS JUST YET. I KNOW IT'S EASY TO DO, BUT YOU'RE STILL UNDER AGE, AND I WORRY.

Panel 7: I'M NOT GOING TO ASK IF YOU WENT INTO THE WINDSOR ARMS PUB. I'M NOT GOING TO ASK IF YOU HAD A BEER OR TWO. I JUST WANTED TO TELL YOU WE ARE CONCERNED. OK?
OK.

Panel 8: SOMETIMES SHE MAKES IT IMPOSSIBLE TO LIE... EVEN IF I **WANTED** TO!!

Panel 9: WHAT DID MOM WANT TO TALK TO YOU PRIVATELY ABOUT, LIZ?
SHE KNOWS I WENT INTO A BAR THE OTHER NIGHT, AN' SHE'S NOT TOO HAPPY ABOUT IT.

Panel 10: YOU **DID?!!**—THAT'S COOL!—WHAT WAS IT LIKE?

Panel 11: WELL, IT WAS SMOKY AND DIRTY AN' A CREEPY OLD GUY TRIED TO PICK UP ONE OF MY FRIENDS. IT WAS PRETTY BORING, ACTUALLY.
YEAH.

Panel 12: ...THAT'S THE TROUBLE WITH A LOT OF STUFF YOU'RE NOT SUPPOSED TO DO!

ON VALENTINE'S DAY, THE WORDS "OPEN UP YOUR HEART" HAVE A WHOLE NEW MEANING!

100

MIKE, YOU REALLY DO LIVE ON PLANET X. HOW ARE YOU GONNA GET MARRIED AND STILL WORK WITH ME?

I WANT TO TRAVEL! I WANT TO SEE THE TAJ MAHAL, I WANT TO PHOTOGRAPH THE SPHINX AND WALK ON THE GREAT WALL OF CHINA!

SO DO I!

WELL, YOU CAN'T DO BOTH!

I KNOW. I'M SO CONFUSED, WEED. I DON'T KNOW WHETHER TO FOLLOW MY HEART OR MY HEAD.

I USUALLY FOLLOW MY HEAD.

THAT'S 'CAUSE IT'S ATTACHED DIRECTLY TO YOUR STOMACH.

WHOA! THIS IS INTERESTING!

WHAT IS IT, A LETTER? WHO'S IT FROM?

PORTRAIT MAGAZINE.

THE PHOTOS AN' STORY WE DID ON THE O'CONNOR FAMILY IS UP FOR AN AWARD. THEY WANT US TO DO A BIGGER STORY!

WHAT?!!

WHEAT PUFFS

THE FAMILY HAS APPROACHED A PUBLISHER. THEY WANT TO KNOW IF WE'D BE WILLING TO TRAVEL TO IRELAND!

IT'S POSTMARKED LAST MONTH

WHEAT

WHY DIDN'T YOU OPEN THIS ENVELOPE AGES AGO?!!

...IT LOOKED LIKE A BILL.

WE'RE UP FOR THE LENS AND LETTERS AWARD, WEED. IT'S GONNA HAPPEN. WE'RE GONNA GO PLACES!

I'VE BEEN HOPING FOR THIS, MIKE. I MEAN, WITH YOU TALKING ABOUT MARRIAGE AN' EVERYTHING, I NEVER THOUGHT YOU'D CUT LOOSE AN' TRAVEL WITH ME!

ARE YOU KIDDING? I AM, LIKE, SO EXCITED ABOUT THIS—I'VE GOTTA CALL MY FOLKS! I'VE GOTTA TELL DEANNA!!

OH, MAN...I'VE GOT TO TELL DEANNA.

HOW CAN I DO THIS? HOW AM I GOING TO TELL DEANNA THAT I HAVE A CHANCE TO TRAVEL AFTER WE GRADUATE?

WE'VE TALKED ABOUT MARRIAGE, BUT WE'VE NEVER SAID WHEN. STILL... I CAN'T IMAGINE BEING WITH ANYONE BUT HER.

BUT OFFERS LIKE THIS DON'T HAPPEN EVERY DAY, SO I GUESS THE BEST THING IS TO COME RIGHT OUT AND SAY...

MICHAEL... I HAVE A CHANCE TO TRAVEL AFTER I GRADUATE.

WE BOTH KNOW WE'RE NOT READY TO GET MARRIED YET. THERE'S LOTS OF TIME.

I WAS OFFERED A JOB AT THE HOSPITAL PHARMACY, BUT I TURNED IT DOWN. I HAVE AN OPPORTUNITY TO GO TO HONDURAS.

HONDURAS?

THEY NEED PHARMACISTS, MICHAEL. THEY NEED DOCTORS AND NURSES AND TEACHERS. I'M VOLUNTEERING TO GO WITH THE MEDICAL MISSIONARIES.

WHEN YOU THINK ABOUT IT ...HOW OFTEN DO YOU HAVE THE CHANCE TO MAKE A DIFFERENCE IN SOMEONE'S LIFE?!

YOU'RE GOING TO HONDURAS! AND I'M SO EXCITED ABOUT IT.

WEED AND I HAVE A CHANCE TO GO TO IRELAND, DEANNA.

I'M NOT SURPRISED. YOU TWO ARE GETTING TO BE QUITE WELL-KNOWN.

JOSEF WEEDER IS AN ARTIST—AND YOU'RE A NOVELIST, MICHAEL... WHETHER YOU KNOW IT OR NOT!

I GUESS I KNOW IT. I JUST DON'T BELIEVE IT YET.

111

Panel 1: SO WHAT ARE THE CHANCES OF OUR WINNING THAT AWARD, WEED? / I DUNNO. THESE THINGS CAN BE POLITICAL. BUT... "NOMINATED" IS NICE.

Panel 2: TO TELL YOU THE TRUTH, I'M MORE EXCITED ABOUT IRELAND! THE O'CONNORS ASKED FOR US SPECIFICALLY. ...PRETTY NICE COMPLIMENT, MAN!

Panel 3: HERE WE ARE, TWO UN-KNOWNS, AN' THEY'RE TRUSTING US TO DO THIS BOOK! I FEEL SERIOUS ENERGY IN THIS, MIKE. / GOOD.

Panel 4: I FEEL SERIOUS TERROR.

Panel 5: I TOLD MY PARENTS I'D SIGNED UP FOR THE MEDICAL MISSION TO HONDURAS, MICHAEL. THEY WEREN'T PLEASED.

Panel 6: I SAID I'LL BE VACCINATED FIRST AND ALL OF OUR FOOD WILL BE SPECIALLY PREPARED— BUT THEY'RE SO AFRAID THAT SOMETHING WILL HAPPEN TO ME.

Panel 7: I TOLD THEM THAT WE TAKE RISKS EVERY DAY! EVERY TIME WE LEAVE OUR HOMES, DRIVE A CAR, CROSS THE STREET! ACCIDENTS HAPPEN! PEOPLE GET MUGGED! / AND?..

Panel 8: THEY SAID IF I WAS GOING TO BE MUGGED... THEY PREFERRED THAT IT BE BY A CANADIAN.

Panel 9: MAYBE YOUR FOLKS THINK YOU SHOULD HAVE ASKED THEM BEFORE YOU AGREED TO GO TO HONDURAS. / THEN WE'D HAVE HAD A REAL PROBLEM.

Panel 10: WELL, I THINK IT'S GREAT THAT YOU'RE GOING TO VOLUNTEER. IT'LL BE A TRULY AMAZING EXPERIENCE. / I KNOW!

Panel 11: I'M GLAD YOU'RE SO SUPPORTIVE, MICHAEL. ...AND I WILL BE HOME FOR CHRISTMAS.

Panel 12: CHRISTMAS?

Panel 1:
TRACEY? MICHAEL!
I CAN'T STAY FOR LONG!

Panel 2:
HERE SHE IS. SAY HELLO TO ROSEMARY.

Panel 3:
GO ON. TAKE HER! HOLD HER!...SHE WON'T BREAK.

Panel 4:
I'M HOLDING YOUR BRAND NEW BABY GIRL! SHE'S REALLY HERE! DOESN'T IT ALL SEEM LIKE A WONDERFUL, MAGICAL MIRACLE?!

Panel 5:
...NOT FROM WHERE I'M SITTING!

Panel 6:
I DROVE HERE SO FAST, I DIDN'T HAVE TIME TO BRING YOU A GIFT OR FLOWERS.
YOU'RE MY PRESENT, OK?

Panel 7:
IN FACT, WE'RE LEAVING THE HOSPITAL TODAY. YOU CAN DRIVE US HOME.
WHAT ABOUT GORDON?

Panel 8:
HE'LL BE HAPPY TO STAY AT THE GARAGE, MICHAEL. HE'S SO BUSY RIGHT NOW ...AND MY FOLKS ARE STILL IN FLORIDA.

Panel 9:
SO, YOU'LL DRIVE US HOME?
TRACEY... IT WOULD BE AN HONOR.

Panel 10:
WE GO RIGHT BY THE GARAGE ON THE WAY TO YOUR HOUSE, TRACE —
LET'S STOP IN! GORD WILL WANT TO SEE YOU.

Panel 11:
I CAN'T BELIEVE I GET TO DRIVE TRACEY AND LITTLE ROSEMARY HOME!
YOU'RE "FAMILY", MIKE!

Panel 12:
WOW! THE EXPANSION IS FINISHED!
UH-HUH. AND WE HAVE A GOOD "PRE-OWNED" CAR SALE BUSINESS AS WELL.

'N'S GARAGE
Service

Panel 13:

IT'S EASY TO BE SUCCESSFUL, MIKE. YOU JUST HAVE TO STARVE A LITTLE, BE GOOD AT WHAT YOU DO... AND WORK YOUR BUTT OFF.

122

WHY ARE YOU TWO BEING SO MISERABLE TO EACH OTHER THIS MORNING?

APRIL HOGS THE SHOWER!

OH, YEAH? WELL, YOU TAKE FOREVER WITH YOUR SPECIAL BUFFY-PUFF AN' YOUR STINKY BODY WASH!

YOU WASTE TIME PLAYING WITH TOYS IN THERE, LIKE IT'S SOME KIND OF FUN HOUSE!!

SNORT

JUST LOOK AT IT THIS WAY, EL...AT LEAST THEY'RE CLEAN!

ELLY! GUESS WHAT! I DID IT!!!

YOU DID WHAT?

OH...OH, YOU DID IT!!

I HAD MY EYES DONE. I GOT THE STITCHES OUT LAST NIGHT AND GREG PICKED ME UP FROM THE CLINIC THIS MORNING!

WOW!

CONNIE, I'M SO EXCITED FOR YOU!

THIS IS MY FIRST EXPERIMENT WITH PLASTIC SURGERY, EL...AND I THINK IT WAS A TOTAL SUCCESS!!

HOW DO I LOOK?

SEE? THEY DID A SORT OF "RUNNING STITCH" AROUND HERE, WHICH THEY TOOK OUT, AND THE STITCHES ALONG THE BOTTOM WILL REABSORB.

I WON'T BE ABLE TO WEAR EYE MAKEUP FOR 4-6 WEEKS, BUT WHO CARES? MY BAGS ARE GONE!

IT WAS AN INTERESTING EXPERIENCE, EL. THERE WERE SEVERAL OF US IN SURGERY AT THE SAME TIME: A NOSE, SOME THIGHS, A LITTLE SILICONE, A LITTLE SUCTION.

IF YOU WANT SOMETHING CHANGED, YOU CAN DO IT!!

CONNIE...I WOULDN'T KNOW WHERE TO BEGIN!